Why I Cry

Burgundy Tears

Testimony and Poetic Writings

Cedrik O. Wallace
Poetic Soldier

Cover designed by Cedrik O. Wallace

Interior by Cedrik O. Wallace

Introduction: My Testimony edited by Maria Dunn Sotelo

Copyright © 2018 Cedrik O. Wallace

All rights reserved.

ISBN: 1729604552
ISBN-13: 978-1729604557

FOR MY POETIC WRITING

follow and contact Cedrik on Instagram
@poeticsoldier

follow and contact Cedrik on Twitter
@cedrikwallace

Cedrik O. Wallace

DEDICATED TO

all cancer warriors, survivors, & caregivers
also all those fighting life battles of any kind

ACKNOWLEDGEMENTS

Thank you to my *family*, friends, the James A. Garfield High School community of East Los Angeles, Kaiser Permanente, City of Hope, the writing community on Instagram, the cancer fighting community, Whittier College, National University, Los Angeles, and God.

You all have played a major role in the healing process as writing has become my therapy. Your continued expertise, encouragement, love, support, and prayers have been a blessing. I'm forever grateful.

No one fights alone.

CONTENTS

1	Introduction	1
2	Purpose	13
3	Meeting Cancer	25
4	The Fight Within	31
5	Side Effects	52
6	The Journey	75
7	Find a Cure	90
8	Live To Inspire	96
9	Surviving Death	112
10	Self Care	127
11	Hospital Visits	147
12	Remedies	152
13	God Listens, Believe Me!	167

Introduction
MY TESTIMONY

Think about this for a second. On Cinco De Mayo, 2012, I watched famed boxer, Floyd Mayweather, win another fight. To this day he still remains undefeated. That may have been a sign of what was to come, for me. The universe speaks loud at times and in some instances, gives subtle clues. Needless to say, we all can agree, it was telling me that a fight of a lifetime was soon coming my way. A major bout! A 'fight to the death' scenario! It is safe to say that the universe was saying to me that I'd soon find my way through some battles and when it was all said and done, I would come out victorious.

With that being said, let me get to my story. On Monday, May 7th, I woke up to that annoying and familiar sound of the alarm clock. The difference this time, was that a sharp pain I felt in my lower back was screaming louder than the clock, as it wouldn't allow me to reach over to shut it up. I finally did, but it was the worst pain I'd ever endured. I could barely get out of bed or even take a shower. Putting on my pants and shoes were a workout within itself. It hurt so bad that I broke out into a sweat. Even though I was late to work, the Capricorn inside of me drove me there. I will never forget the looks on the wide-eyed faces when I first slowly walked into the high school's main office. When their mouths dropped to the floor, it was as if they had seen a ghost.
"Are you feeling ok?" One coworker said.
"You look pale, Mr. Wallace," another loudly whispered.
After disclosing what I was feeling to a co-worker whom I shared the dean's office with, she looked straight into my eyes and told me, "You need to get out of here and go to the doctor!"
That would be my last day of work for almost a year.

As I drove to urgent care at Kaiser Permanente, all I could do was think ahead to getting something to relieve the pain, even if it was temporary. Oddly, my back actually felt better as I drove in my SUV. (I had finally put those fancy seats with the lumbar adjustment controls to good use!) Once I was able to speak to a doctor, she asked me if I had done anything that would strain my back such as lifting, twisting, or falling. I knew for sure I hadn't done anything that would cause injury to my back. She prescribed some Vicodin and ordered me stay home from work for up to three days. She told me that I had probably pulled a muscle and needed to rest my body. After waking up the next several days, in worsening pain, and having to have my brother help me out of the bed each time, I returned to Kaiser. There they insisted that I had done something to cause the pain. They prescribed various pain killers, including Norco, and gave me more time off from work. After the first couple of weeks, Kaiser decided to order an X-ray which resulted in findings of fractures in my lower back. At that point I was directed to the laboratory for blood tests. The pain became more and more unbearable to the point where it had affected my walking, and I was unable to lay on my back or sleep in my bed. While waiting for the results of the blood tests, I found myself sitting up in a chair or on my sofa in the living room to sleep at night. It was the worse situation I've ever found myself in. I did not lay down at all for nearly a month.

    An appointment was scheduled for me to see an oncologist. There the results of my blood tests would be discussed. I didn't think anything of it. I just thought it was routine. I didn't think about it much nor stress about it. For the most part I was a healthy 40 year old man who didn't smoke, was a social drinker, regularly worked out at a gym, and had good eating habits. I never had any major health issues. The bottom line is that I never had any reason to think the worst. Finally I'm sitting there waiting for the oncologist to come in. At that point I'm nervous only because I always get nervous when I'm in a doctor's office, to the point where the nurse has to repeatedly check my blood pressure after instructing me to relax and take deep breaths. The oncologist walks in and introduces herself before sitting in front of me. She asked me if I was made aware of why I was there and what the appointment was about. I really didn't know.

"You may have cancer," the oncologist said after she explained the results of the blood tests. "What?" I asked rhetorically in reply as I sat stunned and frozen. I became speechless. Tears started to form as if it were rain preparing to burst through dark clouds. Finally the tears dropped and I cried for several minutes. My sensitive side had been introduced to the world at that moment. The oncologist sat there in such a caring and professional way as I'm sure she had done many times before. She patiently allowed me to take in the news. I attempted to absorb all of what was going on, but instead the weeping tears exuded extreme denial. All I could think of was that damn "C" word. Questions such as "Am I going to die?" and "Why me?" consumed my thoughts.

The oncologist then told me that the results of the blood tests were all pointing to a blood cancer known as Multiple Myeloma. I had never heard of this cancer before. She went on to explain that it was an incurable but treatable rare blood cancer that affects the bones. I was so confused and felt disoriented. I didn't expect any of this at all! My family does not have a history of cancer. Maybe heart issues, diabetes, and other health issues common to the African American family, but not cancer. No way! As if I had not already been hit with a major blow in my body's mid-section, she went for the knock out when she explained to me that even though everything points to Myeloma, she still needed to make sure, to confirm or unconfirm the cancer. When I asked her what she meant by that, she answered, "I have already set up a Bone Marrow Biopsy with my technician and nurse to take place today, only if you agree." For those of you that don't know what that is…, yes, it's where they stick that long needle in your butt! The purpose is to withdraw marrow from within the bone. She explained what the procedure was and that the results would return in one week. The only thing I remember them saying was something about using a long needle and that they would only be able to numb closer to the surface but that I would feel it once the needle touched the bone. Just the thought of it made my eyes water. At first I wasn't having it at all, but I quickly thought about it and decided that it was best I get it done that day. I didn't want to think about it any longer because then I would change my mind. It was better to get it over with. There was one problem; I was already dealing with the pain in my back.

After getting a pre-procedural shot in my arm, I was all set up for my Bone Marrow Biopsy. In addition to the back pain, I was nervous as hell. How did they expect me to get on this table, lay on my stomach, and position my butt to the their needing? The oncologist and her team had the same questions. Finally they allowed me to lay side ways, bend my legs, and tightly grip the handle rails. So the procedure began. They could only numb so far beneath the surface and warned me that I would feel pain once the needle went through the bone to reach the marrow. Oh my gosh!!! The pain was a different kind of pain, something like a pressure pain. I can't really describe it. It lasted for 5 seconds as that was the amount of time needed to draw enough marrow. It felt like 5 minutes as I screamed like a baby for the entire time they counted down, 5 - 4 - 3 - 2 - 1!

Afterwards an appointment was scheduled for me to return in one week to discuss the results and in the meantime I was prescribed Dexamethasone, a steroid medicine that would start treating the condition even if it wasn't cancer. Now keep in mind, I was by myself. Due to my thinking it was a simple informative doctor's appointment that I was going to, I had gone by myself. No family or friend had accompanied me. The drive home was a lonely one, an emotional one, and a long one. I was driving as fast as I could. I just wanted to get home! Once home, I opened the door, grabbed the first seat I could, and broke down like an old engineless and tireless car. I yelled out to my brother, "I might have cancer!" He ran from the kitchen, where he was washing dishes, and hugged me. It was a long, tearful, and silent hug.

The next several days were awful. I tried not to think about it and stayed optimistic, but it was impossible. It was the beginning of a long week as I waited for the results of the biopsy. A part of me still believed that I would be told that it wasn't cancer. The other part told me the opposite. I had decided not to tell my family until I knew for sure with the exception of my brother who is my best friend, and whom I live with. As the week went on I felt as if my body was deteriorating. I was bent over as I stood because my lower back felt so weak and in pain, I could hardly walk. I started to get a bad cough, I was having irregular bowel movements due to all of the pain medicine I was taking, I was not sleeping, and I was still not laying down. I'm not sure what being dead feels like but if I'd guess, it was this!

One day before my appointment to discuss the biopsy results, I received a phone call from a nurse. She stated she was from the office of oncology and she was calling to schedule an appointment for the next day. I told her that I already had an appointment scheduled. She replied that this was for the "chemotherapy class". At first I was thinking that this was a mistake so I told her that I had not heard from the oncologist, or anyone for that matter, regarding the biopsy results. The nurse got quiet and asked in a stuttering voice, "Oh, you haven't..." I immediately interrupted her and asked, "Does this mean I have cancer?" Before she could answer I said, "Never mind, put the doctor on the phone or please have her call me!!!" Someone at Kaiser had made a horrible mistake. My oncologist did call me back and apologized. She informed me that the results did come back confirming Myeloma and that we needed to proceed with various appointments over the next two days including the chemotherapy class that educates me and my family on everything we needed to know surrounding chemotherapy and my options. What I was going through mentally at that moment would easily define the phrase "mixed-emotions," as I was livid, scared, and confused, all at once.

It was the very next day, June 7th, 2012, exactly a month after waking up in the worse pain imaginable and not being able to lay on my back for an entire month, that I was officially diagnosed with stage three Multiple Myeloma. The symptoms that defined "stage three" included multiple compression fractures in my lower back and my bones were brittle which in part caused me to lose over 2 inches in my height. I spent two days going from the Kaiser Permanente in Bellflower and Downey to the Kaiser Permanente in Hollywood preparing for the bout with cancer all while fighting what I thought was a cold or flu and using a walker to get around. On June 10th, three days after being diagnosed, I went to the emergency room because of a high fever and an uncontrollable cough that was affecting my breathing. It was at that point I knew it was bad. I could feel it as I sat in a wheelchair in the waiting room crying my eyes out. Shortly after being placed in a medical bed, I knocked out. It felt like heaven as the bed held me just right. I was out for hours. After a month of unrestful sleep and not being able to lay on my back, my mind and body were finally able to get some sound sleep as my soul was beginning to wake up again.

I must say, being in that emergency room (ER) was a blessing. The ER nurse did everything she could to make me feel comfortable and assured me that all was going to be ok. It was like she knew something. She understood what I was going through as she shared her own personal experiences about her family. After a night in ER, I was admitted to the hospital with a severe case of pneumonia and other complications. This was a result of an immune system that had shut down due to the Dexamethasone and not taking care of myself properly during the past two days. A few days after being admitted to the hospital, that same nurse came to my room to see how I was doing. When my family told her about my severe pain and how the minimal pain relievers being given were not working, she suggested that we request Dilaudid. A strong pain reliever that doctors don't usually want to prescribe and is given intravenously. She was right. It was a life saver as it better relieved my back pain and allowed me to sleep in peace. To see a nurse step out of the box for the benefit of her patients gave me a sense of hope.

Several days later I almost passed away after my condition worsened and I was transferred to the Intensive Care Unit where I remained for five days. To this day I can't recall many details of that time during my hospital stay. It's as if I'd blacked out and was catching up on all that sleep I had missed out on. My body did not have its counterpart, my willpower, to help with the fight. Maybe that's why I had almost died. In addition to remembering the many visitors from family to co-workers standing around me, holding my hands, praying, and talking to me, to the tubes coming out of my various body parts, one thing has always stood out in my mind. A doctor, I had never seen before, walked into my room in ICU and asked me if I had a family member that could make decisions for me if I was unable to and who would that person be. I remember that because it was the first time I had a male doctor come to see me and he seemed very concerned. However because I was so out of it, I didn't think much of it at the time. At the time I was being discharged from nearly a one month stay in the hospital, the regular doctor said to me, "I can tell you now, it's a miracle that you are here and doing so well, we almost lost you early on."

    After the first two months of my journey I learned that God really does listen. "Team Cedrik" was in full effect as everyone from my family to my work community and everyone between prayed! From prayer circles in my hospital room, churches, to strangers praying from afar on social media. In the summer of 2017, I got a tattoo of prayer hands with the words "God Listens" on my arm to celebrate my 5th year "cancerversary," and to recognize the prayers and support that continue to bless me.

    While in the hospital, I was unable to start chemotherapy due to the pneumonia that had taken over. However, I did five rounds of radiation. I was transported five times from the Kaiser Permanente in Downey to the Kaiser Permanente in Hollywood by ambulance for radiation treatments. They were the most uncomfortable round trips ever taken in my entire life. The EMT's did everything possible to stabilize my back for the ambulance rides, but I felt every bump in the road with tremendous pain. Each round trip was about two hours for only 10 minutes of radiation. I would return to my hospital room each time only to feel nausea and vomit my guts out. Two months following my discharge from the hospital, fluids remained in my lungs. It wasn't until after a thoracentesis was done that I was able to start chemotherapy. Thoracentesis is a procedure where they stick a long needle into my lungs by way of my back, as I sit up bent forward, withdrawing the remaining fluids. I was able to start my chemotherapy shortly thereafter in September 2012. The treatment included Dexamethasone, Revlimid, and infusion treatments of Velcade. Side effects included a weak immune system, fatigue, hot flashes, diarrhea, nausea, vomiting, weakness, and memory loss.

Four months into my fight with cancer and one month of chemotherapy, I'd had my share of a new norm that included being catered to at the hospital, in my own home by my mother, home nurses, an occupational therapist, and a physical therapist. I was restricted from doing anything and my stubborn independent ass wanted to become independent already. My mother was not for that. She wanted dearly to take care of her son and that included not allowing me to do anything, even if I felt ready. She bathed me, fed me, gave me my meds, drove me, and did all of my home duties including laundry and cleaning. My mom had definitely defined the true meaning of caregiver. So in addition to the titles I'd already given her such as Moms and my best friend, she had now become my caregiver. A glance into my daily routine was getting up to my mom's caring and patient voice saying, "Speedy, its time to get up." Yes, you heard that right. Speedy is a nickname she gave to me and has called me since I was a young child. In fact most of my family calls me that name, some with variations to it such as Speedex. The name has something to do with me running around all the time as a child or maybe because I was slow and used to take my time doing everything. Ask her, she'll tell you (laughing). So anyway, back to my daily routine. I'd slowly get up from my medical bed, off-balanced, and walk to the restroom, holding on to whatever I could. After getting ready and eating a light breakfast, I'd grab my walker that my mother had positioned for me or my wheelchair and to say to her, "Let's do this!" before heading out to one of many daily appointments. In my mind, this had become my new life.

If I ever questioned the notion of, "everything happens for a reason," I didn't any more after October, 2012. As I stated above, I was suffocating and being held back in my own home. I was ready to do more but wasn't being allowed to. I wanted to start returning to normalcy. I began blaming those closest to me for the way I was feeling. The fight was no longer in me. I needed to get away. Well, guess what? It turns out that I needed to be out of my home for a brief time due to some home repairs and a new building elevator being installed. I fought it at first, but my mother and brother encouraged me to go for my own good because of my health concerns. I stayed with other family members for a month and, I must say, that was the turning point. During that time I had a lot of time to myself and it was a good thing. I was forced to have some much needed self time. I did some heavy reflecting, strengthened some relationships, and set some short term and long term goals. I had my freedom and began to regain my independence. I knew my limits but also knew my body. I was able to make up my own bed, do some exercise, do my own laundry, and even cooked a little. Wow, everything *does* happen for a reason. Getting away was a retreat of sorts. I felt a sense of former self and I realized then, that I was ready to kick cancer's ass. The fight was on!

My body had responded well to most treatments including a monthly treatment called Zometa, a two-hour intravenous treatment. This would go on for two years and its purpose was to strengthen my bones. Yes, I had some setbacks such as passing out at home and being rushed to the hospital by ambulance, but it all was preparing me for what was to come. By January 18th, 2013, I was in remission. Thereafter I had 8.2 cells collected, enough for two transplants! This included a three-day chemotherapy treatment prior to the collection. That chemo was HELL! I didn't sleep for three days straight because it felt like the cells in my body were pounding on my bones from within to get out. Throbbing PAIN!

After missing nearly a year of work fighting cancer, I had survived the toughest part of my journey. I went back to work and I continue to survive six years later. I'm currently on a maintenance treatment plan, or as I like to call it, "chemo pills", where I hope to remain undefeated. I take one Revlimid capsule per day for 21 days followed by a 7 day rest period. I strive to keep my stress level down, stay positive, eat right, exercise, follow the doctor's orders, pray, and live life. The ongoing side effects can be a nuisance and sometimes overwhelming. Many days consist of chronic fatigue as a result of what my body went through fighting cancer and as a side effect from the treatment used to maintain remission. Everything from the level of activity allowed, to my taste in foods, has changed. Life after cancer is a changed life but the appreciation for it runs deeper than ever. I am so blessed to be alive and *writing* about it.

Purpose

My Purpose

A misconception about me
is that I can help one survive, literally.
However I can't, no really.
What I can do is tell my story.
That's why I write poetry.
With it I can speak to you, openly.
I hope my words help with your journey.

My words are everything
but imaginary.
They are my testimony
through poetry.

Why I Cry

I've become a sensitive man.
I don't care.
If you see me cry,
care.
Don't stare.
Ask.
I will tell you why.

- my first ever written poem

You Asked

You ask me why.
I'll tell you but just know,
you may not be able
to keep your eyes dry.

Burgundy Tears

I picked up a ribbon
to dry my eyes.
The rich color from within
absorbed into the
piece of cloth, like dye.
Releasing the pain from inside
was necessary after my fight.
The healing began thereafter,
letting go through my cry.

- a burgundy ribbon represents
  Multiple Myeloma cancer

Truth Heals

A **healing** truth is spoken
when written words
come from a place that's broken.

Down my cheeks came tears
because of emotional fear.
At times they turned into cheers
because of the love from far and near.
At times I still cry and people hear
but they understand loud and clear.

You wipe my tears
as I cry,
showing me that I'm not alone
when I fight.
This takes me home,
the only place that feels right.

Until Next Year

This year has come to an end.
To the new year I must befriend.
What comes my way I will apprehend,
hold on to, and not give up or give in.
Until its purpose I know and comprehend
I'll utilize it until the countdown happens again.

- happy new year

Purposely

What is the purpose
was the purpose.
A purpose
done on purpose
for me to realize my purpose.

My body took major hits
and my mind had many fits.
The heart remained in high spirits
and instead of giving in to dying
my soul was purifying.
A purpose filled the mold
and my story of survival was told.

- crucible of cancer

Meeting Cancer

Waiting

An upset stomach,
not the kind you think,
but from the nerves
thinking about what's to come.

C Word

you want to know what i did
when i first heard
it was scary hearing that word
so let me tell you
i cried for a half hour before
the doctor could continue

Meeting Cancer

When I first met him,
he shook my hand
with a viciously firm grip,
sending extreme shock waves
through my body.
How else do you expect
me to respond to,
"My name is Cancer.
It's nice to meet you.
How are you doing?"

Cancer

He is a true terrorist
who is not a racist.
He doesn't commit suicide
for us to suffer and die.
He tortures and watches
as we count our losses.

*- a revised version of my original poem
   published in POETICA By Me Poetry, 2017*

What the Hell?

I thought I had died
and gone to hell.
Then again I hadn't done
anything to end up there.

The Fight Within

Be defined
by the strength and courage
it takes to fight this,
not by the dirty way
this battle
is fought by the illness.

Sometimes
life will hit you
out of nowhere.
Swing back!
Hit back!
It's more than fair.

Reality Hits

I realized "oh shit!"
when that illness hit.
I had always taken my
health for granted
until fighting for my
life was demanded.

Invite It

Your mind and body
begs of your soul to fight.
The warrior within you
just needs an invite.

Let's Do This

I was scared to death.
That was all I needed
to fight for my health.

Lost & Found

Never say never.
When it comes
down to it, we seem
to find that strength
we once thought
was lost forever.

Fight and continue.
Life will be good to you.

I Will

Let me tell you how I feel.
You, the murderer, I will kill.
Your momentum I will steal
and I will continue to heal.
Just know I am for real
and I will seal the deal.

Fuck You Cancer

You I will defy
because I am not your fall-guy.
You will not be the reason I die.
No matter how hard you try
my will to live remains very high.

No two battles are alike,
yet what determines the
same outcome is the fight.

It gets to a point
where you just go
through the motions
to get through.
The passion *will* return
when it's due.
That, **I promise you**.

If I Die

You came into my life.
I was already here and that's our strife.
Therefore you are fighting me.
I'm not fighting you, which is key.
Try to take me out.
I promise this will be your toughest bout.

Moment

It's surreal
what you feel
when they go in
for the kill.
Either you fight
or you kneel.

Desire

When an internal
fighting threat
breaks out into
a welcoming sweat.

Trust me to put my all into it
even though I'm not physically fit.
I will go through the motions
on the strength of my emotions.

My mind you tried to use
as for my body you did abuse.
My soul you tried to seduce
as for *your* control I did reduce.

our will to fight it
makes us survivors
even if in the end
the cancer takes our lives

- *survivor*

Last Shot

Fighting for my last breath
will be like, 3-2-1 buzzer.
A winning shot before my death
in a battle like no other.

MVP

Life is like a sport
Fighting battles of all sorts
Always treat it as a home game
Yet the outcome depends on your aim
With your effort and focus to win each play
Giving it your all is always a win on game day

i stay swinging and i stay ducking
maybe that is why i am exhausted
to stay alive i have to keep fighting

Cedrik O. Wallace

Side Effects

Imprisoned

My body took a huge hit
after pain killers lined my stomach.
My bloated belly no longer fit
and forever I couldn't take a shit.
Not until a week into my hospital visit
the doctors were finally able to free it.

Insanity

Deep sleep
allows me to keep
my sanity.
While meds creep,
my energy they sweep
is the reality.
With a price not cheap,
they are the black sheep
in the family.
I wake up and leap
just to repeat
insanely.

Body Shots

I'll never forget the needles
breaking through the skin of my love handles,
causing my bruised stomach to look
and feel as if they were man handled.

- velcade chemotherapy injections

Brain On Drugs

Known for my great memory
Now it has become my enemy
Remembering things from way back
Recalling yesterday's conversation I now lack
Everything cancer took from me I've mostly regain
What I continue to struggle with is this chemo brain

- chemo brain is real

For us
with chemo brain,
it's such a pain.

It's real, this chemo brain,
trying to keep up and maintain.
To remember is a **memorable** pain.

Fatigue

The years following my fight,
at times, has made me bow.
True exhaustion has never been, until now.
The body loses fuel quickly and breaks down.
Whatever it went through during those rounds,
it hasn't been able to regain ground.
Only true sleep and daily naps
allow temporary rebound.

I can feel the difference.
These meds sure do bring
such a unique tiredness.

Pain

If you've had your cells harvested,
you know what I'm talking about.
The pain from the pre-collection chemotherapy
was unlike the previous bout.
It felt like little creatures were pounding
from within my bones to get out.
A very aggressive chemo for three straight days.
I didn't sleep at all and I could do was pray.
Oh God, I begged, please make it go away.

Sexiety

For my body you go
going for what you know.
In my attempt to reload
you must take it slow.
Unlike my soul
my body has lost its glow.

3 a.m.

Time for the after party.
Not the kind you think.
Cramps goes through my body
as I stumble pass the sink.
To the toilet awaits hardly.
Life at that point quickly stinks.
I return feeling like I'm crawling.
All due to a treatment-to-live link.

- body cramps, nausea, and diarrhea

It makes me such a hot mess
knowing there is a connection
between cancer and stress.

- a correlation between stress and cancer

Before cancer I was always wired.
Now my body feels as if it is differently wired.
Knowing what it went through.
I often ask, "Why am I so tired?"
My body is just simply tired.

I am tired
of being tired.

"That's Okay"

My mom
reminded me that
there is nothing wrong
with the fact
that sometimes
I don't feel strong.

Today was a down day
which only means that
tomorrow will go my way.

A Good Day

I wish I felt this way
every single day.
You know, like a child
who jumps out of bed,
leaving it unfurled
and has all of the energy
to take on the world.

- that rare day of no pain and high energy

Today,
I'm just
trying to be
comfortable.
Anything
less is
insufferable.

Side Effects

They usually
have their way.
At least for today
the cramps, fatigue,
and hot flashes,
have gone away.
I just wish
they wouldn't return
any other day.

I'm so blessed
to wake up.
To have received
rest is a plus.

Living with tiredness and pain
yet who am I to complain.
Bad days come and go
but it's the good that grows.
It may be my new norm
however I remain in living form.

It has made
my body feel old
but at the same time
it has been
good for the soul.

The Journey

Realize

The realization
of your progress
comes from your journey
through the process.

That Part

Through it all
we fall and rise.
It is a **journey**
we must endure
until our demise.

To accomplish
it all
one must rise after
each fall.

I fell to true depths
and up invisible ladders
I did rise again

Faith

The only way to overcome this,
is to have faith.
So allow a miracle to do its thing
and at its own pace.

Going into a low point
is never appealing
but when you first come out of it,
it's the best feeling.

Brought down
temporarily by pain.
Getting back up
constantly,
leads to life gains.

A Strong Finish

Your strength will always outweigh the weak.
With it, you will come out with a victory,
even if it's a comeback from underneath.

V.I.P.

Having to face and
overcome hard times
makes us more valuable
when in our prime.

- valuable in prime

Just Know

I don't care who you are
Go ahead and dare to know my scars
Pretend to understand what I've been through
Just know you have no clue
On a witness stand you'd be lying
If one would to start prying
Here is the answer
You haven't had cancer

The Journey

Don't settle for what is minimal.
The road to your dreams will be phenomenal.
With ups, downs, or not quite getting there.
What you accomplish will be more than fair.

make the best
of your journey
and the best will come

Cedrik O. Wallace

through all of your challenges
finding what's true will be **YOU**

It *Just* Hit Me

When asked
what positive things
came from my journey with cancer,
I can say I have several answers.
However this writing stuff
came out of no where,
like when the cancer
just hit me out of no where.

Cedrik O. Wallace

Find a Cure

I smell a tantalizing aroma.
It's the spreading of hope
to find a cure for Multiple Myeloma.

?

Why have they not
found a cure
Is all that money
for research pure

No Cure

When fighting a battle,
one will ask *the question*.
Unfortunately some
will not find the answer.
Take me for instance.
In my case it is due
to me battling cancer.

Epidemic

What the fuck.
This is just too much.
Another person with cancer.
We need an answer.
It's so infuriating
to see it escalating.

Ok, now you know I got the will
and I'm so over this chemo pill.
I'm ready to completely heal.
Let's stop playing and bring the cure!

Live To Inspire

Life is king
where a breath is queen.
To wear your crown
you must live by all means.

Living with a sense of gratitude
will be reflected in your attitude
and observed by others in great magnitude.

A duty of ours
while living
is to inspire others
into believing.

Keep pushing forward
to where you want to stay
and inspire as many people
as you can on the way.

Man Power

Through my pores,
my experiences have ran.
From the core
sprints a man.
Proving, 'I know I can'
get back up and stand.
That's why I'm a fan
of the rewarding energy
that comes from inspiration.
In form of will power.
Like rays from the sun
causing perspiration
to thirst quenching at happy hour.

- inspired

I'm on cloud nine
because I'm still alive.
Try to interfere with mine.
You'll only motivate me to thrive.

Make It Rain

A little rain
never hurt nobody
as I sit atop cloud nine
in good spirits
letting it all out,
sprinkling reason.

Life is a trip at times
but it's at such times
you have to get back up
and keep living.

It's
all right,
I was given
another
chance at life.

Cedrik O. Wallace

Life is nothing but a dream
It's everything if we live it

Time is
borrowed
not given.
So pay it back
by living.

Live Life

When asked if life is
treating you well,
first, ask yourself if
you are living it to
the fullest. In return
your answer will tell.

fam*ILY*

My backbone
and my inspiration
are all intact.
Without you,
I don't know what I'd do.
It is a simple fact.
Fam, *I love you.*

Last Meal

Before it is my time to go,
cooking in an incinerator,
please butterfly my whole.
Send my body up the escalator
and leave behind my spirit's role.
This may defy the plan of my creator
but inspiring others was my goal
and well done it'll be as their savior.

Live To Inspire

Not giving up, that's you.
So inspiring,
it's true.
You I'm admiring,
makes me continue.
Living life not retiring,
I hope to inspire someone too.

Cedrik O. Wallace

Surviving Death

Not Now

The room is dim
not shining so bright.
They want me to join them
wishing to turn off my lights.
I will not go unless it's him
who says that the time is right.

I'm a Survivor

Diagnosed with cancer.
Going into survival mode was my answer.
What other choice did I have in the matter.
I mean that was all I thought about.
Not if I survived but how I'd go out.
Going through the process I was surviving.
Fighting and living life is what I wasn't depriving.
Losing the fight rather it's short term or long term,
never imply the word *survivor* wasn't earned.
We all die at some point don't we?
Rather it's due to cancer or being cancer-free.

He's always willin'
to seek a spirit for the stealin'.
Not mine as i'm not chillin'
with high action and energy.
Defeating the villain
like the end of a movie.
Surviving each scene.
This story will end
in a victory that will only mean
I'm the villain in his story,
stealing his glory
physically and mentally.

- defeating cancer

Mid Life Crisis

Driving down my path,
I was struck with a crisis at mid life.
Scared to death I wouldn't survive.
So strange because this cancer strikes at average 65.
However twenty five years younger for me,
this must have been a sign.
A miracle, good health, young age, or a positive attitude,
I was going to shine.
A fight to the death, I would win.
Sure enough, as any man having a mid life crisis,
I'm driving down my path again.
Taking my new car for a spin.

*- purchasing a new car during my second
year in remission inspired this piece*

I am here
I am alive
but I fear
I question
how long
I will survive

It's not about
surviving cancer.
It's about overcoming
the fear of death.
Understanding that,
you will have already survived.

Afterlife

My eyes fill with tears
because the unknowns of my exit, I fear.
Yet, feelings of joy appear,
knowing what's beyond the next entrance, is clear.

Good Night's Rest

Today you look into my eyes
and see that I'm just too tired to fight.
Yet you see that I'm blind to the idea of dying,
knowing what comes after tonight.

True Soldier

I'm a fighter.
I fight with confidence.
I believe in what I'm fighting for.
My weapons of choice
are activity, clean eating,
vitamins, and prescribed medicine.
My shield is made of a positive attitude.
My energy is fueled by rest,
my passion for life, and faith.
My supporters and I are killing the enemy
with prayers and a smile.
I survive the war by living life.

Life sees that
I've come along way
as **death** sees that
I have a long way to go.

Ha Ha, Sike!

I almost shook hands with death
but decided to leave him hanging.

Cancer,
you suck
I'm still here
and it's not by luck.
Merely a sign that
you are fucked!

another survivor
weakens cancer

Fight & Teach

What I do for a living.
I impact adults and children.
I live life everyday
to express my appreciation for its way.
My fight for life is the juice.
Working and playing hard has a truce
because I strive to be present for awhile.
However, if I ever die,
my absence will be noticeable
for miles and miles.
Leaving behind a spiritual presence
as well as a difference.

Self Care

Oh I do care.
However I think
looking after
my health first, is fair.

Retreat

Like a flower, it's
important to close
up and get away
It brings out a
deeper inner beauty
when it awakes.

Do you for you
in every case.
All else will fall
into its very place.

Self Love

Look into my eyes, in depth
They say love yourself
A broken heart I've felt
Maybe I caused myself
I'm good now for that book is on the shelf
I've learned to first love thyself
My happiness is my true wealth
Today it's me, myself, and good health

Wait.
Take a break.
Keep your life awake.
It's fate.
God's plan is never late.

I do this for self gain.
Writing emotion and sharing experienced pain.
A self-seeking purpose to inspire others
as some uninvited agendas hovers.
Reciprocating those advances to grant a wish
but to continue a healthy prognosis,
I may need to be a bit more selfish.

Let go
of what's heavy
because it's
weighing you down.

It doesn't matter
what you did
and what you're doing.
Place your bid
and keep going.

Try to let go
and start a new,
everyday.

Tomorrow

Work hard to get through today
and you will reap the rewards
of what tomorrow will pay.

Take a seat
You look beat
Use the
down time
and prepare to defeat
before raising to your feet

Rest and reflection.
Building on this
will be my protection.

Pause for a minute.
Take a look around.
Inhale your blessings.
Exhale the bullshit.
Now continue on.

Accept that
you're blessed,
nothing less.

My Eyes

Looking out the windows of my mind
I never know what I will find
Sometimes it's there but it's as if I'm blind
So wiping my views or washing them with a tear
My thoughts that are blurry will become clear
In return my reality will no longer be tinted with fears

Trust in yourself
and your inner strength
will grow to become
your own unbreakable shelter.

Peace & Love

As your own witness,
loving yourself
and choosing happiness
will do wonders for your mental health.
The stress and negativity that's released
will bring you inner peace.

Dear Negativity:

Somehow you got hired.
Soon you'll be replaced or fired
because your energy is undesired.
If not, my energy will eventually
have you retired.

Your Superior,
Positivity

My Birthday

On this born day
add another candle.
What comes my way
I will be able to handle.

Hospital Visits

Hope

No way!
This is better than any horoscope.
My nurse in the ER said her name was Hope.
It was at that moment I knew I'd cope.
That is exactly what she gave me, a new scope.

Waiting Room

Sitting here waiting
for my oncologist
reminds me of the day
I first met her.
The day she gave me
the news that
I couldn't digest.

Doctor's Office

I'm waiting in this room
as tools and sorts loom.
However in my mind,
anticipating her words consume.

At the hospital, a lot of time I'm spending.
My home away from home, it's becoming.
However, it's where **I'm making a living**.

Cedrik O. Wallace

Remedies

My Prescription

Poetry acts as a bottle of meds
that need to be time-released to heal.
The prescribed words refill
as treatment runs out and pain returns.

Writing to heal.
For each appeal,
a layer I will peel.

The battle I fought was traumatic.
The life I live after can be hectic.
The art it inspires is healing and poetic.

Venting

I'm not acting out of despite.
Instead I was inspired to write.
I have no ill will towards
what I didn't invite.
However when in my feelings,
through words, I fight.

Truth

Art is so uniquely innocent
but guilty of reflecting
an individual's inner reality.

Deep

My deep experiences
lead to deeper thoughts
and through writing the
meaning in depth is caught.

When my eyes are closed
I see the story that will be written.
Inspired thoughts pose
as the words snap a picture.

Day Off

What has captured me
is that today I feel free.
Letting go of last week
and replacing it with where I want to be.
Using the time to speak
through the words I leak.
My reflection explained before you seek.
Just know I am blessed for tomorrow I will see.

Get a glimpse of my mind
through the words in my rhyme.

A Song

I will use it
and get lost
in the music.
Escaping from a life
that can be abusive.

Your
healing
comedy
laughs
at
my
other
remedies.

- laughter is good for the soul

Again,
poetry
is
the
remedy.

Poetic Soldier

During my journey
I was inspired to write
through the eyes of a warrior
who had fought and survived.

- *my username on Instagram*

Poetic Fight

People say love not war.
What about the love for life
that's in the hearts core.
In this case war is the answer.
It's all good if I bleed
during this fight with cancer.
The blood from my wounds
The tears from my moods.
As long as I'm living…
both will spill out in words.
Writing about what I'm going through
and what my life can afford.

God Listens, Believe Me!

Don't talk
about what happened
unless it had you and God
doing some serious interacting.

Pray

Talk to your God
whoever he may be.
To you he will nod
and that will be key.

His Touch

Allow God's hand in all
His footsteps beside you
If needed his strength to carry you
Talk to him and he will listen
What I'm saying is pray
Or not
Either way
You will always feel his touch

I pray to god
I know he is listening
Evil prays to the devil
who is the enemy
He must be hard of hearing
because I'm still winning

He The Devil

He came up with a for sure killer plan,
though he thought.
Cancer was supposed to make anyone fold.
At first, killing all those who fought.
Instead it made the true warriors more bold.
Prayer and the right attitude they caught,
as if it was a contagious cold.
He who challenged God to a war forgot
that our healer in mind, body, and soul,
will dare the devil to take his best shot.

When prayers came
overwhelmingly
with love from the community
in such unity,
that was the moment I realized
that I was loved by so many.

God Listens

To you I appeal,
as I heal.
Believe me I have felt,
as the hearts around me melt.
You listen when they pray.
Oh, thank you Lord.
I'm here to stay.

God's Plan

My life span
is in his hands
and with his plan
that will always stand.
I have no choice
but to be a fan.
Yet I did choose my path
and with it I've ran.

Forward I face.

Not looking over my shoulder,
I pace.
You do have my back.
I trust.
To turn around
is not a must.

Thanksgiving

I can't begin to express
my overwhelming gratitude
as the support, love, and prayers
you all give have continued.

My appreciation will be shown
by fighting with a positive attitude.

Again, thanks for giving.
It's because of you, I'm living.

- forever grateful

5/7/12

That day I woke up.
I wish I hadn't.
The pain was too much.
Not knowing what happened.

Today I wake up.
Happy the line didn't flatten.
It's a miracle not luck.
All I went through and what happened.

Miracle

I know you may feel misled.
You saw me on my deathbed
and now you see me moving ahead.
Just know it was your prayers
that came through instead.

- i am the Magic Johnson of cancer

They ask
why I smile.
I simply answer,
I'm alive.

Made in the USA
Middletown, DE
05 March 2019